The Gospel of Wealth

Andrew Carnegie

The Gospel of Wealth

By Andrew Carnegie

1889

I. THE PROBLEM OF THE ADMINISTRATION OF WEALTH

THE problem of our age is the proper administration of wealth, that the ties of brotherhood may still bind together the rich and poor in harmonious relationship. The conditions of human life have not only been changed, but revolutionized, within the past few hundred years. In former days there was little difference between the dwelling, dress, food, and environment of the chief and those of his retainers. The Indians are to-day where civilized man then was. When visiting the Sioux, I was led to the wigwam of the chief. It was like the others in external appearance, and even within the difference was trifling between it and those of the poorest of his braves. The contrast between the palace of the millionaire and the cottage of the laborer with us to-day measures the change which has come with civilization. This change, however, is not to be deplored, but welcomed as highly beneficial. It—is well, nay, essential, for the progress of the race that the houses of some should be homes for all that is highest and best in literature and the arts, and for all the refinements of civilization, rather than that none should be so. Much better this great irregularity than universal squalor. Without wealth there can be no Mæcenas. The "good old times" were not good old times. Neither master nor servant was as well situated then as to-day. A relapse to old conditions would be disastrous to both-not the least so to him who serves-and would sweep away civilization with it. But whether the change be for good or ill, it is upon us, beyond our power to alter, and, therefore, to be accepted and made the best of. It is a waste of time to criticize the inevitable.

It is easy to see how the change has come. One illustration will serve for almost every phase of the cause. In the manufacture of products we have the whole story. It applies to all combinations of human industry, as stimulated and enlarged by the inventions of this scientific age. Formerly, articles were manufactured at the domestic hearth, or in small shops which formed part of the household. The master and his apprentices worked side by side, the latter living with the master, and therefore subject to the same conditions. When these apprentices rose to be masters, there was little or no change in their mode of life, and they, in turn, educated succeeding apprentices in the same routine. There was, substantially, social equality, and even political equality, for those engaged in industrial pursuits had then little or no voice in the State.

The inevitable result of such a mode of manufacture was crude articles at high prices. To-day the world obtains commodities of excellent quality at prices which even the preceding generation would have deemed incredible. In the commercial world similar causes have produced similar results, and the race is benefited thereby. The poor enjoy what the rich could not before afford. What were the luxuries have become the necessaries of life. The laborer has now more comforts than the farmer had a few generations ago. The farmer has more luxuries than the landlord had, and is more richly clad and better housed. The landlord has books and pictures rarer and appointments more artistic than the king could then obtain.

The price we pay for this salutary change is, no doubt, great. We assemble thousands of operatives in the factory, and in the mine, of whom the employer can know little or nothing, and to whom he is little better than a myth. All intercourse between them is at an end. Rigid castes are formed, and, as usual, mutual ignorance breeds mutual distrust. Each caste is without sympathy with the other, and ready to credit anything disparaging in regard to it. Under the law of competition, the employer of thousands is forced into the strictest economies, among which the rates paid to labor figure prominently, and often there is friction between the employer and the employed, between capital and labor, between rich and poor. Human society loses homogeneity.

The price which society pays for the law of competition, like the price it pays for cheap comforts and luxuries, is also great; but the advantages of this law are also greater still than its cost-for it is to this law that we owe our wonderful material development, which brings improved conditions in its train. But, whether the law be benign or not, we must say of it, as we say of the change in the conditions of men to which we have referred: It is here; we cannot evade it; no substitutes for it have been found; and while the law may be sometimes hard for the individual, it is best for the race, because it insures the survival of the fittest in every department. We accept and welcome, there fore, as conditions to which we must accommodate ourselves, great inequality of environment; the concentration of business, industrial and commercial, in the hands of a few; and the law of competition between these, as being not only beneficial, but essential to the future progress of the race. Having accepted these, it follows that there must be great scope for the exercise of special ability in the merchant and in the manufacturer who has to conduct affairs upon a great scale. That this talent for organization and management is rare among men is proved by the fact that it invariably secures enormous rewards for its possessor, no matter where or under what laws or conditions. The experienced in affairs always rate the man whose services can be obtained as a partner as not only the first consideration, but such as render the question of his capital scarcely worth considering: for able men soon create capital; in the hands of those without the special talent required, capital soon takes wings. Such men become interested in firms or corporations using millions; and, estimating only simple interest to be made upon the capital invested, it is inevitable that their income must exceed their expenditure and that they must, there fore, accumulate wealth. Nor is there any middle ground which such men can occupy, because the great manufacturing or commercial concern which does not earn at least interest upon its capital soon becomes bankrupt. It must either go forward or fall behind; to stand still is impossible. It is a condition essential to its successful operation that it should be thus far profitable, and even that, in addition to interest on capital, it should make profit. It is a law, as certain as any of the others named, that men possessed of this peculiar talent for affairs, under the free play of economic forces must, of necessity, soon be in receipt of more revenue than can be judiciously expended upon them selves; and this law is as beneficial for the race as the others.

Objections to the foundations upon which society is based are not in order, because the condition of the race is better with these than it has been with any other which has been tried. Of the effect of any new substitutes proposed we cannot be sure. The Socialist or Anarchist who seeks to overturn present conditions is to be regarded as attacking the foundation upon which civilization itself rests, for civilization took its start from the day when the capable, industrious workman said to his incompetent and lazy fellow, "If thou cost not sow, thou shalt not reap," and thus ended primitive Communism by separating the drones from the bees. One who studies this subject will soon be brought face to face with the conclusion that upon the sacredness of property civilization itself depends-the right of the laborer to his hundred dollars in the savings-bank, and equally the legal right of the millionaire to his millions. Every man must be allowed "to sit under his own vine and fig-tree, with none to make afraid," if human society is to advance, or even to remain so far advanced as it is. To those who propose to substitute Communism for this intense Individualism, the answer therefore is: The race has tried that. All progress from that barbarous day to the present time has resulted from its displacement. Not evil, but good, has come to the race from the accumulation of wealth by those who have had the ability and energy to produce it. But even if we admit for a moment that it might be better for the race to discard its present foundation, Individualism,-that it is a nobler ideal that man should labor, not for himself alone, but in and for a brotherhood of his fellows, and share with them all in common, realizing Swedenborg's idea of heaven, where, as he says, the angels derive their happiness, not from laboring for self, but for each other, - even admit all this, and a sufficient answer is, This is not evolution, but revolution. It necessitates the changing of human nature itself-a work of eons, even if it were good to change it, which we cannot know.

It is not practicable in our day or in our age. Even if desirable theoretically, it belongs to another and long-succeeding sociological stratum. Our duty is with what is practicable now-with the next step possible in our day and generation. It is criminal to waste our energies in endeavoring to uproot, when all we can profitably accomplish is to bend the universal tree of humanity a little in the direction most favorable to the production of good fruit under existing circumstances. We might as well urge the destruction of the highest existing type of man because he failed to reach our ideal as to favor the destruction of Individualism, Private Property, the Law of Accumulation of Wealth, and the Law of Competition; for these are the high est result of human experience, the soil in which society, so far, has produced the best fruit. In equally or unjustly, perhaps, as these laws some times operate, and imperfect as they appear to the Idealist, they are, nevertheless, like the highest type of man, the best and most valuable of all that humanity has yet accomplished.

We start, then, with a condition of affairs under which the best interests of the race are promoted, but which inevitably gives wealth to the few. Thus far, accepting conditions as they exist, the situation can be surveyed and pronounced good. Question then arises.-and if the foregoing be correct, it is the only question with which we have to deal,-What is the proper mode of administering wealth after the laws upon which civilization is founded have thrown it into the hands of the few.7 And it is of this great question that I believe I offer the true solution. It will be under stood that fortunes are here spoken of, not moderate sums saved by many years of effort, the returns from which are required for the comfortable maintenance and education of families. This is not wealth, but only competence, which it should be the aim of all to acquire, and which it is for the best interests of society should be acquired.

There are but three modes in which surplus wealth can be disposed of. It can be left to the families of the decendents; or it can be bequeathed for public purposes; or, finally, it can be administered by its possessors during their lives. Under the first and second modes most of the wealth of the world that has reached the few has hitherto been applied. Let us in turn consider each of these modes. The first is the most injudicious. In monarchical countries, the estates and the greatest portion of the wealth are left to the first son, that the vanity of the parent may be gratified by the thought that his name and title are to descend unimpaired to succeeding generations. The condition of this class in Europe to-day teaches the failure of such hopes or ambitions. The successors have become impoverished through their follies, or from the fall in the value of land. Even in Great Britain the strict law of entail has been found inadequate to maintain an hereditary class. Its soil is rapidly passing into the hands of the stranger. Under republican institutions the division of property among the children is much fairer; but the question which forces itself upon thoughtful men in all lands is, Why should men leave great fortunes to their children. If this is done from affection, is it not misguided affection. Observation teaches that, generally speaking, it is not well for the children that they should be so burdened. Neither is it well for the State. Beyond providing for the wife and daughters moderate sources of income, and very moderate allowances indeed, if any, for the sons, men may well hesitate; for it is no longer questionable that great sums bequeathed often work more for the injury than for- the good of the recipients. Wise men will soon conclude that, for the best interests of the members of their families, and of the State, such bequests are an improper use of their means.

It is not suggested that men who have failed to educate their sons to earn a livelihood shall cast them adrift in poverty. If any man has seen fit to rear his sons with a view to their living idle lives, or, what is highly commendable, has instilled in them the sentiment that they are in a position to labor for public ends without reference to pecuniary considerations, then, of course, the duty of the parent is to see that such are provided for in moderation. There are instances of millionaires' sons unspoiled by wealth, who, being rich, still perform great services to the community. Such are the very salt of the earth, as valuable as, unfortunately, they are rare. It is not the exception however, but the rule, that men must regard; and, looking at the usual result of enormous sums conferred upon legatees, the thoughtful man must shortly say, "I would as soon leave to my son a curse as the almighty dollar," and admit to himself that it is not the welfare of the children, but family pride, which inspires these legacies.

As to the second mode, that of leaving wealth at death for public uses, it may be said that this is only a means for the disposal of wealth, provided a man is content to wait until he is dead before he becomes of much good in the world. Knowledge of the results of legacies bequeathed is not calculated to inspire the brightest hopes of much posthumous good being accomplished by them. -The cases are not few in which the real object sought by the testator is not attained, nor are they few in which his real wishes are thwarted. In many cases the bequests are so used as to be come only monuments of his folly. It is well to remember that it requires the excercise of not less ability than that which acquires it, to use wealth so as to be really beneficial to the community Besides this, it may fairly be said that no man is to be extolled for doing what he cannot help doing, nor is he to be thanked by the community to which he only leaves wealth at death. Men who leave vast sums in this way may fairly be thought men who would not have left it at all had they been able to take it with them. The memories of such cannot be held in grateful remembrance,-for there is no grace in their gifts. It is not to be wondered at that such bequests seem so generally to lack the blessing.

The growing disposition to tax more and more heavily large estates left at death is a cheering indication of the growth of a salutary change in public opinion. The State of Pennsylvania now takes-subject to some exceptions-one tenth of the property left by its citizens. The budget presented in the British Parliament the other day proposes to increase the death duties; and, most significant of all, the new tax is to be a graduated one. Of all forms of taxation this seems the wisest. Men who continue hoarding great sums all their lives, the proper use of which for public ends would work good to the community from which it chiefly came, should be made to feel that the community, in the form of the State, cannot thus be deprived of its proper share. By taxing estates heavily at death the State marks its condemnation of the selfish millionaire's unworthy life.

It is desirable that nations should go much further in this direction. Indeed, it is difficult to set bounds to the share of a rich man's estate which should go at his death to the public through the agency of the State, and by all means such taxes should be graduated, beginning at nothing upon moderate sums to dependents, and increasing rapidly as the amounts swell, until of the millionaire's hoard, as of Shylock's, at least

> The other half
> Comes to the privy coffer of the State.

This policy would work powerfully to induce the rich man to attend to the administration of wealth during his life, which is the end that society should always have in view, as being by far the most fruitful for the people. Nor need it be feared that this policy would sap the root of enterprise and render men less anxious to accumulate, for, to the class whose ambition it is to leave great fortunes and be talked about after their death, it will attract even more attention, and, indeed, be a somewhat nobler ambition, to have enormous sums paid over to the State from their fortunes.

There remains, then, only one mode of using great fortunes; but in this we have the true antidote for the temporary unequal distribution of wealth, the reconciliation of the rich and the poor -a reign of harmony, another ideal, differing, indeed, from that of the Communist in requiring only the further evolution of existing conditions, not the total overthrow of our civilization. It is founded upon the present most intense Individual ism, and the race is prepared to put it in practice by degrees whenever it pleases. Under its sway we shall have an ideal State, in which the surplus wealth of the few will become, in the best sense, the property of the many, because administered for the common good; and this wealth, passing through the hands of the few, can be made a much more potent force for the elevation of our race than if distributed in small sums to the people themselves. Even the poorest can be made to see this, and to agree that great sums gathered by some of their fellow-citizens and spent for public purposes, from which the masses reap the principal benefit, are more valuable to them than if scattered among themselves in trifling amounts through the course of many years.

If we consider the results which flow from the Cooper Institute, for instance, to the best portion of the race in New York not possessed of means, and compare these with those which would have ensued for the good of the masses from an equal sum distributed by Mr. Cooper in his lifetime in the form of wages, which is the highest form of distribution, being for work done and not for charity, we can form some estimate of the possibilities for the improvement of the race which lie embedded in the present law of the accumulation of wealth. Much of this sum, if distributed in small quantities among the people, would have been wasted in the indulgence of appetite, some of it in excess, and it may be doubted whether even the part put to the best use, that of adding to the comforts of the home, would have yielded results for the race, as a race, at all comparable to those which are flowing and are to flow from the Cooper Institute from generation to generation. Let the advocate of violent or radical change ponder well this thought.

We might even go so far as to take another instance-that of Mr. Tilden's bequest of five millions of dollars for a free library in the city of New York; but in referring to this one cannot help saying involuntarily: How much better if Mr. Tilden had devoted the last years of his own life to the proper administration of this immense sum; in which case neither legal contest nor any other cause of delay could have interfered with his aims. But let us assume that Mr. Tilden's millions finally become the means of giving to this city a noble public library, where the treasures of the world contained in books will be open to all forever, without money and without price. Considering the good of that part of the race which congregates in and around Manhattan Island, would its permanent benefit have been better promoted had these millions been allowed to circulate in small sums through the hands of the masses! Even the most strenuous advocate of Communism must entertain a doubt upon this subject. Most of those who think will probably entertain no doubt what ever.

Poor and restricted are our opportunities in this life, narrow our horizon, our best work most imperfect; but rich men should be thankful for one inestimable boon. They have it in their power during their lives to busy themselves in organizing benefactions from which the masses of their fellows will derive lasting advantage, and thus dignify their own lives. The highest life is probably to be reached, not by such imitation of the life of Christ as Count Tolstoi gives us, but, while animated by Christ's spirit, by recognizing the changed conditions of this age, and adopting modes of expressing this spirit suitable to the changed conditions under which we live, still laboring for the good of our fellows, which was the essence of his life and teaching, but laboring in a different manner.

This, then, is held to be the duty of the man of wealth: To set an example of modest, unostentatious living, shunning display or extravagance; to provide moderately for the legitimate wants of those dependent upon him;

and, after doing so, to consider all surplus revenues which come to him simply as trust funds, which he is called upon to administer, and strictly bound as a matter of duty to administer in the manner which, in his judgment, is best calculated to produce the most beneficial results for the community-the man of wealth thus becoming the mere trustee and agent for his poorer brethren, bringing to their service his superior wisdom, experience, and ability to administer, doing for them better than- they would or could do for themselves.

We are met here with the difficulty of determining what are moderate sums to leave to members of the family; what is modest, unostentatious living; what is the test of extravagance. There must be different standards for different conditions. The answer is that it is as impossible to name exact amounts or actions as it is to define good manners, good taste, or the rules of propriety; but, nevertheless, these are verities, well known, although indefinable. Public sentiment is quick to know and to feel what offends these. So in the case of wealth. The rule in regard to good taste in the dress of men or women applies here. Whatever makes one conspicuous offends the canon. If any family be chiefly known for display, for extravagance in home, table, or equipage, for enormous sums ostentatiously spent in any form upon itself-if these be its chief distinctions, we have no difficulty in estimating its nature or culture. So likewise in regard to the use or abuse of its surplus wealth, or to generous, free handed cooperation in good public uses, or to unabated efforts to accumulate and hoard to the last, or whether they administer or bequeath. The verdict rests with the best and most enlightened public sentiment. The community will surely judge, and its judgments will not often be wrong.

The best uses to which surplus wealth can be put have already been indicated. Those who would administer wisely must, indeed, be wise; for one of the serious obstacles to the improvement of our race is indiscriminate charity. It were better for mankind that the millions of the rich were thrown into the sea than so spent as to encourage the slothful, the drunken, the unworthy. Of every thousand dollars spent in so-called charity to-day, it is probable that nine hundred and fifty dollars is unwisely spent-so spent, indeed, as to produce the very evils which it hopes to mitigate or cure. A well-known writer of philosophic books admitted the other day that he had given a quarter of a dollar to a man who approached him as he was coming to visit the house of his friend. He knew nothing of the habits of this beggar, knew not the use that would be made of this money, although he had every reason to suspect that it would be spent improperly. This man professed to be a disciple of Herbert Spencer; yet the quarter-dollar given that night will probably work more injury than all the money will do good which its thought less donor will ever be able to give in true charity. He only gratified his own feelings, saved himself from annoyance-and this was probably one of the most selfish and very worst actions of his life, for in all respects he is most worthy.

In bestowing charity, the main consideration: should be to help those who will help themselves; to provide part of the means by which those who desire to improve may do so; to give those who desire to rise the aids by which they may rise; to assist, but rarely or never to do all. Neither the individual nor the race is improved by almsgiving. Those worthy of assistance, except in rare cases, seldom require assistance. The really valuable men of the race never do, except in case of accident or sudden change. Every one has, of course, cases of individuals brought to his own knowledge where temporary assistance can do genuine good, and these he will not overlook. But the amount which can be wisely given by the individual for individuals is necessarily limited by his lack of knowledge of the circumstances connected with each. He is the only true reformer who is as careful and as anxious not to aid the unworthy as he is to aid the worthy, and, perhaps, even more so, for in almsgiving more injury is probably done by rewarding vice than by relieving virtue.

The rich man is thus almost restricted to following the examples of Peter Cooper, Enoch Pratt of Baltimore, Mr. Pratt of Brooklyn, Senator Stanford, and others, who know that the best means of benefiting the community is to place within its reach the ladders upon which the aspiring can rise-free libraries, parks, and means of recreation, by which men are helped in body and mind; works of art, certain to give pleasure and improve the public taste; and public institutions of various kinds, which will improve the general condition of the people; in this manner returning their surplus wealth to the mass of their fellows in the forms best calculated to do them lasting good.

Thus is the problem of rich and poor to be solved. The laws of accumulation will be left free, the laws of distribution free. Individualism will continue, but the millionaire will be but a trustee for the poor, intrusted for a season with a great part of the increased wealth of the community, but administering it for the community far better than it could or would have done for itself. The best minds will thus have reached a stage in the development of the race in which it is clearly seen that there is no mode of disposing of surplus wealth creditable to thoughtful and earnest men into whose hands it cows, save by using it year by year for the general good. This day already dawns. Men may die without incurring the pity of their fellows, still sharers in great business enterprises from which their capital cannot be or has not been withdrawn, and which is left chiefly at death for public uses; yet the day is not far distant when the man who dies leaving behind him millions of available wealth, which was free for him to administer during life, will pass away "unwept, unhonored, and unsung," no matter to what uses he leaves the dross which he cannot take with him. Of such as these the public verdict will then be: " The man who dies thus rich dies disgraced."

Such, in my opinion, is the true gospel concerning wealth, obedience to which is destined some day to solve the problem of the rich and the poor, and to bring "Peace on earth, among men good will."

II. THE BEST FIELDS FOR PHILANTHROPY

WHILE "The Gospel of Wealth" has met a cordial reception upon this side of the Atlantic, it is natural that in the motherland it should have attracted more attention, because the older civilization is at present brought more clearly face to face with socialistic questions. The contrast between the classes and the masses, between rich and poor, is not yet quite so sharp in this vast, fertile, and developing continent, with less than twenty persons per square mile, as in crowded little Britain, with fifteen times that number and no territory unoccupied. Perhaps the "Pall Mall Gazette" in its issue of September 5 puts most pithily the objections that have been raised to what the English have been pleased to call "The Gospel of Wealth." 1 I quote: " Great fortunes, says Mr. Carnegie, are great blessings to a community, because such and such things may be done with them. Well, but they are also a great curse, for such and such things are done with them. Mr. Carnegie's preaching, in other words, is altogether vitiated by Mr. Benzon's practice. The gospel of wealth is killed by the acts."

To this the reply seems obvious: the gospel of Christianity is also killed by the acts. The same objection that is urged against the gospel of wealth lies against the commandment, "Thou shalt not steal." It is no argument against a gospel that it is not lived up to ,indeed it is an argument in its favor, for a gospel must be higher than the prevailing standard. It is no argument against a law that it is broken: in that disobedience lies the reason for making and maintaining the law; the law which is never to be broken is never required.

Undoubtedly the most notable incident in regard to " The Gospel of Wealth " is that it was fortunate enough to attract the attention of Mr. Gladstone, and bring forth the following note from him: "I have asked Mr. Lloyd Bryce ["North American Review"] kindly to allow the republication in this 1 this article appeared originally under the title "Wealth." country of the extremely interesting article on 'Wealth,' by Mr. Andrew Carnegie, which has just appeared in America." This resulted in the publication of the article in several newspapers and periodicals, and an enterprising publisher issued it in pamphlet form, dedicated by permission to Mr. Gladstone.

All this is most encouraging, proving as it does that society is alive to the great issue involved, and is in a receptive mood. Your request, Mr. Editor, that I should continue the subject and point out the best fields for the use of surplus wealth, may be taken as further proof that whether the ideas promulgated are to be received or rejected, they are at least certain to obtain a hearing.

The first article held that there is but one right mode of using enormous fortunes-namely, that the possessors from time to time during their own lives should so administer these as to promote the permanent good to the communities from which they were gathered. It was held that public sentiment would soon say of one who died possessed of available wealth which he was free to administer: " The man who dies thus rich dies disgraced."

The purpose of this paper is to present some of the best methods of performing this duty of administering surplus wealth for the good of the people. The first requisite for a really good use of wealth by the millionaire who has accepted the gospel which proclaims him only a trustee of the surplus that comes to him, is to take care that the purposes for which he spends it shall not have a degrading pauperizing tendency upon its recipients, but that his trust shall be so administered as to stimulate the best and most aspiring poor of the community to further efforts for their own improvement. It is not the irreclaimably destitute, shiftless, and worthless which it is truly beneficial or truly benevolent for the individual to attempt to reach and improve. For these there exists the refuge provided by the city or the State, where they can be sheltered, fed, clothed, and kept in comfortable existence, and-most important of all-where they can be isolated from the well-doing and industrious poor, who are liable to be demoralized by contact with these unfortunates. One man or woman who succeeds in living comfortably by begging is more dangerous to society, and a greater obstacle to the progress of humanity, than a score of wordy Socialists. The individual administrator of surplus wealth has as his charge the industrious and ambitious; not those who need everything done for them, but those who, being most anxious and able to help themselves, deserve and will be benefited by help from others and by the extension of their opportunies by the aid of the philanthropic rich.

It is ever to be remembered that one of the chief obstacles which the philanthropist meets in his efforts to do real and permanent good in this world, is the practice of indiscriminate giving and the duty of the millionaire is to resolve to cease giving to objects that are not clearly proved to his satisfaction to be deserving. He must remember Mr. Rice's belief, that nine hundred and fifty out of every thousand dollars bestowed to-day upon so-called charity had better be thrown into the sea. As far as my experience of the wealthy extends, it is unnecessary to urge them to give of their superabundance in charity so called. Greater good for the race is to be achieved by inducing them to cease impulsive and injurious giving. As a rule, the sins of millionaires in this respect are not those of omission, but of commission, because they do not take time to think, and chiefly because it is much easier to give than to refuse. Those who have surplus wealth give millions every year which produce more evil than good, and really retard the progress of the people, because most of the forms in vogue to-day for benefiting mankind only tend to spread among the poor a spirit of dependence upon alms, when what is essential for progress is that they should be inspired to depend upon their own exertions. The miser millionaire who hoards his wealth does less injury to society than the careless millionaire who squanders his unwisely, even if he does so under cover of the mantle of sacred charity. The man who gives to the individual beggar commits a grave offense, but there are many societies and institutions soliciting alms, to aid which is none the less injurious to the community. These are as corrupting as individual beggars Plutarch's "Morals" contains this lesson: " A beggar asking an alms of a Lacedaemo- nian, he said:—'- Well, should I give thee anything, thou wilt be the greater beggar, for he that first gave thee money made thee idle, and is the cause of this base and dishonorable way of living.' As I know them, there are few millionaires, very few indeed, who are clear of the sin of having made beggars.

Bearing in mind these considerations, let us endeavor to present some of the best uses to which a millionaire can devote the surplus of which he should regard himself as only the trustee.

First. Standing apart by itself there is the founding of a university by men enormously rich, such men as must necessarily be few in any country. Perhaps the greatest sum ever given by an individual for any purpose is the gift of Senator Stanford, who undertakes to establish a complete university upon the Pacific coast, where he amassed his enormous fortune, which is said to involve the expenditure of ten millions of dollars, and upon which he may be expected to bestow twenty millions of his surplus. He is to be envied. A thousand years hence some orator, speaking his praise upon the then crowded shores of the Pacific, may thus adapt Griffith's eulogy of Wolsey:

> In bestowing, madam,
> He was most princely. Ever witness for him
> This seat of learning, . . .

though unfinished, yet so famous,
So excellent in art, and still so rising,
That Christendom shall ever speak his virtue.

Here is a noble use of wealth. We have many such institutions,-Johns Hopkins, Cornell, Packer, and others,- but most of these have only been bequeathed, and it is impossible to extol any man greatly for simply leaving what he cannot take with him. Cooper and Pratt and Stanford, and others of this class, deserve credit and admiration as much for the time and attention given during their lives as for their expenditure upon their respective monuments.

We cannot think of the Pacific coast without recalling another important work of a different character which has recently been established there -the Lick Observatory. If any millionaire be interested in the ennobling study of astronomy,-and there should be and would be such if they but gave the subject the slightest attention,-here is an example which could well be followed, for the progress made in astronomical instruments and appliances is so great and continuous that every few years a new telescope might be judiciously given to one of the observatories upon this continent, the last being always the largest and the best, and certain to carry further and further the knowledge of the universe and of our relation to it here upon the earth. As one among many of the good deeds of the late Mr. Thaw of Pittsburg, his constant support of the observatory there may be mentioned. This observatory enabled Professor Langley to make his wonderful discoveries. He is now at the head of the Smithsonian Institution, a worthy successor to Professor Henry. Connected with him was Mr. Braeshier of Pittsburg, whose instruments are in most of the principal observatories of the world. He was a common millwright but Mr. Thaw recognized his genius and was his main support through trying days. This common workman has been made a professor by one of the foremost scientific bodies of the world. In applying part of his surplus in aiding these two now famous men, the millionaire Thaw did a noble work. Their joint labors have brought great credit, and are destined to bring still greater credit, upon their country in every scientific center throughout the world.

It is reserved for very few to found universities, and, indeed, the use for many, or perhaps any, new universities does not exist. More good is henceforth to be accomplished by adding to and extend- ing those in existence. But in this department a wide field remains for the millionaire as distinguished from the Craesus among millionaires. The gifts to Yale University have been many, but there is plenty of room for others. The School of Fine Arts, founded by Mr. Street, the Sheffield Scientific School, endowed by Mr. Sheffield, and Professor Loomis's fund for the observatory, are fine examples. Mrs. C. J. Osborne's building for reading and recitation is to be regarded with especial pleasure as being the wise gift of a woman. Harvard University has not been forgotten; the Peabody Museum and the halls of Wells, Matthews, and Thayer may be cited. Sever Hall is worthy of special mention, as showing what a genius like Richardson could do with the small sum of a hundred thousand dollars. The Vanderbilt University, at Nashville, Tennessee, may be mentioned as a true product of the gospel of wealth. It was established by the members of the Vanderbilt family during their lives-mark this vital feature, during their lives; for nothing counts for much that is left by a man at his death. Such funds are torn from him, not given by him. If any millionaire be at a loss to know how to accomplish great and indisputable good with his surplus, here is a field which can never be fully occupied, for the wants of our universities increase with the development of the country.

Second. The result of my own study of the question, What is the best gift which can be given to a community? is that a free library occupies the first place, provided the community will accept and maintain it as a public institution, as much a part of the city property as its public schools, and, indeed, an adjunct to these. It is, no doubt, possible that my own personal experience may have led me to value a free library beyond all other forms of beneficence. When I was a working-boy in Pittsburg, Colonel Anderson of Allegheny-a name I can never speak without feelings of devotional gratitude-opened his little library of four hundred books to boys. Every Saturday afternoon he was in attendance at his house to exchange books. No one but he who has felt it can ever know the intense longing with which the arrival of Saturday was awaited, that a new book might be had. My brother and Mr. Phipps, who have been my principal business partners through life, shared with me Colonel Anderson's precious generosity, and it was when reveling in the treasures which he opened to us that I resolved, if ever wealth came to me, that it should be used to establish free libraries, that other poor boys might receive opportunities similar to those for which we were indebted to that noble man.

Great Britain has been foremost in appreciating the value of free libraries for its people. Parliament passed an act permitting towns and cities to establish and maintain these as municipal institutions; whenever the people of any town or city voted to aacept the provisions of the act, the authorities were authorized to tax the community to the extent of one penny in the pound valuation Most of the towns already have free libraries under this act. Many of these are the gifts of rich men, whose funds have been used for the building, and in some cases for the books also, the communities being required to maintain and to develop the libraries. And to this feature I attribute most of their usefulness. An endowed institution is liable to become the prey of a clique. The public ceases to take interest in it, or, rather, never acquires interest in it. The rule has been violated which requires the recipients to help themselves. Everything has been done for the community instead of its being only helped to help itself, and good results rarely ensue.

Many free libraries have been established in our country, but none that I know of with such wisdom as the Pratt Library in Baltimore. Mr. Pratt built and presented the library to the city of Baltimore, with the balance of cash handed over; the total cost was one million dollars, upon which he required the city to pay five per cent. per annum, fifty thousand dollars per year, to trustees for the maintenance and development of the library and its branches. During 1888 430,217 books were distributed; 37,196 people of Baltimore are registered upon the books as readers. And it is safe to say that 37,000 frequenters of the Pratt Library are of more value to Baltimore, to the State, and to the country, than all the inert, lazy, and hopelessly poor in the whole nation. And it may further be safely said that, by placing books within the reach of 37,000 aspiring people which they were anxious to obtain, Mr. Pratt has done more for the genuine progress of the people than has been done by all the contributions of all the millionaires and rich people to help those who cannot or will not help themselves. The one wise administrator of his surplus has poured a fertilizing stream upon so,1 that was ready to receive it and return a hundredfold. The many squanderers have not only poured their streams into sieves which can never be filled-they have done worse: they have poured them into stagnant sewers that breed the diseases which most afflict the body politic. And this is not all. The million dollars of which Mr. Pratt has made so grand a use are something, but there is something greater still. When the fifth branch library was opened in Baltimore, the speaker said:

"Whatever may have been done in these four years, it is my pleasure to acknowledge that much, very much, is due to the earnest interest, the wise counsels, and the practical suggestions of Mr. Pratt. He never seemed to feel that the mere donation of great wealth for the benefit of his fellow-citizens was all that would be asked of him, but he wisely labored to make its application as comprehensive and effective as possible. Thus he constantly lightened burdens that were, at times, very heavy, brought good cheer and bright sunshine when clouds flitted across the sky, and made every officer and employee feel that good work was appreciated, and loyal dovotion to duty would receive hearty commendation."

This is the finest picture I have ever seen of any of the millionaire class. As here depicted, Mr. Pratt is the ideal disciple of the gospel of wealth. We need have no fear that the mass of toilers will fail to recognize in such as he their best leaders and their most invaluable allies; for the problem of poverty and wealth, of employer and employed, will be practically solved whenever the time of the few is given, and their wealth is administered during their lives, for the best good of that portion of the community which has not been burdened with the responsibilities which attend the possession of wealth. We shall have no antagonism between classes when that day comes, for the high and the low, the rich and the poor, shall then indeed be brothers.

No millionaire will go far wrong in his search for one of the best forms for the use of his surplus who chooses to establish a free library in any community that is willing to maintain and develop it. John Bright's words should ring in his ear: " It is impossible for any man to bestow a greater benefit upon a young man than to give him access to books in a free library." Closely allied to the library, and, where possible, attached to it, there should be rooms for an art-gallery and museum, and a hall for such lectures and instruction as are provided in the Cooper Union. The traveler upon the Continent is surprised to find that every town of importance has its art-gallery and museum; these may be large or small, but each has a receptacle for the treasures of the locality, in which are constantly being placed valuable gifts and bequests. The Free Library and Art Gallery of Birmingham are remarkable among such institutions, and every now and then a rich man adds to their value by presenting books, fine pictures, or other works of art. All that our cities require, to begin with, is a proper fire-proof building. Their citizens who travel will send to it rare and costly things from every quarter of the globe they visit, while those who remain at home will give or bequeath to it of their treasures. In this way collections will grow until our cities will ultimately be able to boast of permanent exhibitions from which their own citizens will derive incalculable benefit, and which they will be proud to show to visitors. In the Metropolitan Museum of Art in New York we have made an excellent beginning. Here is another avenue for the proper use of surplus wealth.

Third. We have another most important department in which great sums can be worthily used-the founding or extension of hospitals, medical colleges, laboratories, and other institutions connected with the alleviation of human suffering, and especially with the prevention rather than with the cure of human ills. There is no danger in pauperizing a community in giving for such purposes, because such institutions relieve temporary ailments or shelter only those who are hopeless invalids.

What better gift than a hospital can be given to a community that is without one -the gift being conditioned upon its proper maintenance by the community in its corporate capacity. If hospital accommodation already exists, no better method for using surplus wealth can be found than in making additions to it. The late Mr. Vanderbilt's gift of half a million dollars to the Medical Department of Columbia College for a chemical laboratory was one of the wisest possible uses of wealth. It strikes at the prevention of disease by penetrating into its causes. Several others have established such laboratories, but the need for them is still great.

If there be a millionaire in the land who is at a loss what to do with the surplus that has been committed to him as trustee, let him investigate the good that is flowing from these chemical laboratories. No medical college is complete without its laboratory. As with universities, so with medical colleges: it is not new institutions that are required, but additional means for the more thorough equipment of those that exist. The forms that benefactions to these may wisely take are numerous, but probably none is more useful than that adopted by Mr. Osborne when he built a school for training female nurses at Bellevue College. If from all gifts there flows one half of the good that comes from this wise use of a millionaire's surplus, the most exacting may well be satisfied. Only those who have passed through a lingering and dangerous illness can rate at their true value the care, skill, and attendance of trained female nurses. Their employment as nurses has enlarged the sphere and influence of woman. It is not to be wondered at that a senator of the United States, and a physician distinguished in this country for having received the highest distinctions abroad, should recently have found their wives in this class.

Fourth. In the very front rank of benefactions public parks should be placed, always provided that the community undertakes to maintain, beautify, and preserve them inviolate. No more useful or more beautiful monument can be left by any man than a park for the city in which he was born or in which he has long lived, nor can the community pay a more graceful tribute to the citizen who presents it than to give his name to the gift. Mrs. Schenley's gift last month of a large park to the city of Pittsburg deserves to be noted. This lady, although born in Pittsburg, married an English gentleman while yet in her teens. It is forty years and more since she took up her residence in London among the titled and the wealthy of the world's metropolis, but still she turns to the home of her childhood and by means of Schenley Park links her name with it forever. A noble use this of great wealth by one who thus becomes her own administrator. If a park be already provided, there is still room for many judicious gifts in connection with it. Mr. Phipps of Allegheny has given conservatories to the park there, which are visited by many every day of the week, and crowded by thousands of working-people every Sunday for, with rare wisdom, he has stipulated as a condition of the gift that the conservatories shall be open on Sundays. The result of his experiment has been so gratifying that he finds himself justified in adding to them from his surplus, as he is doing largely this year. To lovers of flowers among the wealthy I commend a study of what is possible for them to do in the line of Mr. Phipps's example; and may they please note that Mr. Phipps is a wise as well as a liberal giver, for he requires the city to maintain these conservatories, and thus secures for them forever the public ownership, the public interest, and the public criticism of their management. Had he undertaken to manage and maintain them, it is probable that popular interest in the gift would never have been awakened.

The parks and pleasure-grounds of small towns throughout Europe are not less surprising than their libraries, museums, and art-galleries. I saw nothing more pleasing during my recent travels than the hill at Bergen, in Norway. It has been converted into one of the most picturesque of pleasure-grounds; fountains, cascades, waterfalls, delightful arbors, fine terraces, and statues adorn what was before a barren mountain-side. Here is a field worthy of study by the millionaire who would confer a lasting benefit upon his fellows. Another beautiful instance of the right use of wealth in the direction of making cities more and more attractive is to be found in Dresden. The owner of the leading paper there bequeathed its revenues forever to the city, to be used in beautifying it. An art committee decides, from time to time, what new artistio feature is to be introduced, or what hideous feature is to be changed, and as the revenues accrue, they are expended in this direction. Thus, through the gift of this patriotic newspaper proprietor his native city of Dresden is fast becoming one of the most artistic places of residence in the whole world. A work having been completed, it devolves upon the city to maintain it forever. May I be excused if I commend to our millionaire newspaper proprietors the example of their colleague in the capital of Saxony.

Scarcely a city of any magnitude in the older countries is without many structures and features of great beauty. Much has been spent upon ornament, decoration, and architectural effect. We are still far behind in these things upon this side of the Atlantic. Our Republic is great in some things-in material development unrivaled; but let us always remember that in art and in the finer touches we have scarcely yet taken a place. Had the exquisite Memorial Arch recently erected temporarily in New York been shown in Dresden, the art committee there would probably have been enabled, from the revenue of the newspaper given by its owner for just such purposes, to order its permanent erection to adorn the city forever.1

While the bestowal of a park upon a community will be universally approved as one of the best uses for surplus wealth, in embracing such additions to it as conservatories, or in advocating the building of memorial arches and works of adornment, it is probable that many will think I go too far, and consider these somewhat fanciful. The material good to flow from them may not be so directly visible; but let not any practical mind, intent only upon material good, depreciate the value of wealth given for these or for kindred esthetic purposes as being useless as far as the mass of the people and their needs are concerned. As with libraries and museums, so with these more distinctively artistic works: they perform their greatest when they reach the best of the masses of the people. It is better to reach and touch the sentiment for beauty in the naturally bright minds of this class than to pander to those incapable of being so touched. For what the improver of the race must endeavor is to reach those who have the divine spark ever so feebly developed, that it may be strengthened and grow. I Popular subscriptions have Monument), and two other me- accompliahed this result in the morial arches have been designed case referred to (the Washington and are to be erected here.- ED

For my part, I think Mr. Phipps put his money to better use in giving the working-men of Allegheny conservatories filled with beautiful flowers, orchids, and aquatic plants, which they, with their wives and children, can enjoy in their spare hours, and upon which they can feed their love for the beautiful, than if he had given his surplus money to furnish them with bread; for those in health who cannot earn their bread are scarcely worth considering by the individual giver, the care of such being the duty of the State. The man who erects in a city a conservatory or a truly artistia arch, statue, or fountain, makes a wise use of his surplus. " Man does not live by bread alone."

Fifth. We have another good use for surplus wealth in providing our cities with halls suitable for meetings of all kinds, and for concerts of elevating music. Our cities are rarely possessed of halls for these purposes, being in this respect also very far behind European cities. Springer Hall, in Cincinnati, a valuable addition to the city, was largely the gift of Mr. Springer, who was not content to bequeath funds from his estate at death, but gave during his life, and, in addition, gave- what was equally important-his time and business ability to insure the successful results which have been achieved. The gift of a hall to any city lacking one is an excellent use for surplus wealth for the good of a community. The reason why the people have only one instructive and elevating, or even amusing, entertainment when a dozen would be highly beneficial, is that the rent of a hall, even when a suitable hall exists, which is rare, is so great as to prevent managers from running the risk of financial failure. If every city in our land owned a hall which could be given or rented for a small sum for such gatherings as a committee or the mayor of the city judged advantageous, the people could be furnished with proper lectures, amusements, and concerts at an exceedingly small cost. The town halls of European cities, many of which have organs, are of inestimable value to the people, utilized as they are in the manner suggested. Let no one underrate the influence of entertainments of an elevating or even of an amusing character, for these do much to make the lives of the people happier and their natures better. If any millionaire born in a small village which has now become a great city is prompted in the day of his success to do something for his birthplace with part of his surplus, his grateful remembrance cannot take a form more useful than that of a public hall with an organ, provided the city agrees to maintain and use it.

Sixth. In another respect we are still much behind Europe. A form of beneficence which is not uncommon there is providing swimming-baths for the people. The donors of these have been wise enough to require the city benefited to maintain them at its own expense, and as proof of the contention that everything should never be done for any one or for any community, but that the recipients should invariably be called upon to do a part, it is significant that it is found essential for the popular success of these healthful establishments to exact a nominal charge for their use. In many cities, however, the school-children are admitted free at fixed hours upon certain days; different hours being fixed for the boys and the girls to use the great swimming-baths, hours or days being also fixed for the use of these baths by women. In addition to the highly beneficial effect of these institutions upon the public health in inland cities, the young of both sexes are thus taught to swim. Swimming clubs are organized, and matches are frequent, at which medals and prizes are given. The reports published by the various swimming- bath establishments throughout Great Britain are filled with instances of lives saved because those who fortunately escaped shipwreck had been taught to swim in the baths; and not a few instances are given in which the pupils of certain bathing establishments have saved the lives of others. If any disciple of the gospel of wealth gives his favorite city large swimming and private baths, provided the municipality undertakes their management as a city affair, he will never be called to account for an improper use of the funds intrusted to him.

Seventh. Churches as fields for the use of surplus wealth have purposely been reserved until the last, because, these being sectarian, every man will be governed in his action in regard to them by his own attachments; therefore gifts to churches, it may be said, are not, in one sense, gifts to the community at large, but to special classes. Nevertheless every millionaire may know of a district where the little cheap, uncomfortable, and altogether unworthy wooden structure stands at the cross-roads, in which the whole neighborhood gathers on Sunday, and which, independently of the form of the doctrines taught, is the center of social life and source of neighborly feeling. The administrator of wealth makes a good use of a part of his surplus if he replaces that building with a permanent structure of brick, stone, or granite, up whose sides the honeysuckle and columbine may climb, and from whose tower the sweet-tolling bell may sound. The millionaire should not figure how cheaply this structure can be built, but how perfect it can be made. If he has the money, it should be made a gem, for the educating influence of a pure and noble specimen of architecture, built, as the pyramids were built, to stand for ages, is not to be measured by dollars. Every farmer's home, heart and mind in the district will be influenced by the beauty and grandeur of the church; and many a bright boy, gazing enraptured upon its richly colored windows and entranced by the celestial voice of the organ, will there receive his first message from and in spirit be carried away to the beautiful and enchanting realm which lies far from the material and prosaic conditions which surround him in this workaday world- a real world, this new realm, vague and undefined though its boundaries be. Once within its magic circle, its denizens live there an inner life more precious than the external, and all their days and all their ways, their triumphs and their trials, and all they see, and all they hear, and all they think, and all they do, are hallowed by the radiance which shines from afar upon this inner life, glorifying everything, and keeping all right within. But having given the building, the donor should stop there; the support of the church should be upon its own people. There is not much genuine religion in the congregation or much good to come from the church which is not supported at home.

Many other avenues for the wise expenditure of surplus wealth might be indicated. I enumerate but a few-a very few-of the many fields which are open, and only those in which great or considerable sums can be judiciously used. It is not the privilege, however, of millionaires alone to work for or aid measures which are certain to benefit the community. Every one who has but a small surplus above his moderate wants may share this privilege with his richer brothers, and those without surplus can give at least a part of their time, which is usually as important as funds, and often more so.

It is not expected, neither is it desirable, that there should be general concurrence as to the best possible use of surplus wealth. For different men and different localities there are different uses. What commends itself most highly to the judgment of the administrator is the best use for him, for his heart should be in the work. It is as important in administering wealth as it is in any other branch of a man's work that he should be enthusiastically devoted to it and feel that in the field selected his work lies.

Besides this, there is room and need for all kinds of wise benefactions for the common weal. The man who builds a university, library, or laboratory performs no more useful work than he who elects to devote himself and his surplus means to the adornment of a park, the gathering together of a collection of pictures for the public, or the building of a memorial arch. These are all true laborers in the vineyard. The only point required by the gospel of wealth is that the surplus which accrues from time to time in the hands of a man should be administered by him in his own lifetime for that purpose which is seen by him, as trustee, to be best for the good of the people. To leave at death what he cannot take away, and place upon others the burden of the work which it was his own duty to perform, is to do nothing worthy. This requires no sacrifice, nor any sense of duty to his fellows.

Time was when the words concerning the rich man entering the kingdom of heaven were regarded as a hard saying. To-day, when all questions are probed to the bottom and the standards of faith receive the most liberal interpretations the startling verse has been relegated to the rear to await the next kindly revision as one of those things which cannot be quite understood, but which, meanwhile, it is carefully to be noted, are not to be understood literally. But is it so very improbable that the next stage of thought is to restore the doctrine in all its pristine purity and force, as being in perfect harmony with sound ideas upon the subject of wealth and poverty, the rich and the poor, and the contrasts everywhere seen and deplored? In Christ's day, it is evident, reformers were against the wealthy. It is none the less evident that we are fast recurring to that position to-day; and there will be nothing to surprise the student of sociological development if society should soon approve the text which has caused so much anxiety: " It is easier for a camel to enter the eye of a needle than for a rich man to enter the kingdom of heaven." Even if the needle were the small casement at the gates, the words betoken serious difficulty for the rich. It will be but a step for the theologian from the doctrine that he who dies rich dies disgraced, to that which brings upon the man punishment or deprivation hereafter.

The gospel of wealth but echoes Christ's words. It calls upon the millionaire to sell all that he hath and give it in the highest and best form to the poor by administering his estate himself for the good of his fellows, before he is called upon to lie down and rest upon the bosom of Mother Earth. So doing, he will approach his end no longer the ignoble hoarder of useless millions; poor, very poor indeed, in money, but rich, very rich, twenty times a millionaire still, in the affection, gratitude, and admiration of his fellow-men, and- sweeter far-soothed and sustained by the still, small voice within, which, whispering, tells him that, because he has lived, perhaps one small part of the great world has been bettered just a little. This much is sure: against such riches as these no bar will be found at the gates of Paradise.

Printed in the United Kingdom by
Lightning Source UK Ltd., Milton Keynes
138004UK00002BA/4/P